ANIMALS AT WATER'S EDGE

GALLERY BOOKS
An Imprint of W. H. Smith Publishers Inc.
112 Madison Avenue
New York City 10016

This edition first published in U.S.
in 1990 by Gallery Books,
an imprint of W.H. Smith Publishers, Inc.
112 Madison Avenue, New York, New York 10016

ISBN 0-8317-9587-5

Printed and bound in Spain

For rights information about the photographs in
this book please contact:

The Image Bank
111 Fifth Avenue, New York, N.Y. 10003

Producer: Solomon M. Skolnick
Author: Scott Weidensaul
Design Concept: Leslie Ehlers
Designer: Ann-Louise Lipman
Editor: Madelyn Larsen
Production: Valerie Zars
Photo Researcher: Edward Douglas
Design Assistant: Kristi Jo McKnight
Assistant Photo Researcher: Robert Hale

Title page:
**Shrouded in morning mists, a flock of
great egrets hunts for fish, frogs and small
snakes in the shallows of Everglades
National Park, Florida.**

Water is a natural magnet for wildlife. Whether it is a waterhole on the arid African plains, a tropical estuary or a marsh in the Rocky Mountain foothills, the greatest concentrations and diversity of animal life will be found nearby. More than simply the lure of moisture, watery habitats have an abundance of food and shelter. It is no wonder animals seek them out and make them their home.

The water's fringe takes many forms – coastline, pond or lake shore, or wooded bog. Particularly teeming with life are marshes, or wetlands. They serve as nursery, not just to waterfowl, but to thousands of species of animals. Inland marshes and swamps are natural water filters (some communities now use man-made wetlands to treat sewage), and act like giant sponges during torrential rains, absorbing huge quantities of water and letting it out slowly, preventing downstream flooding.

Top to bottom: Poised and ready, an Alaskan brown bear waits for sockeye salmon. The bear must be fast to snag the racing fish, and most attempts end in frustrating misses, but with the vast number of migrating salmon coming upstream, a patient bear is bound to catch a meal – as does this bruin.

Above: In the thick of the salmon run, a brown bear may eat only the egg sacs in each fish, leaving the rest on the shore. Gulls, eagles and foxes clean up the leftovers. *Left:* Once considered a separate species because of its great size, the Alaskan brown bear is now thought to be the same as the interior grizzly. Its massive bulk is due to a rich food supply, including annual salmon runs. *Opposite:* Surrounded by the splendor of the autumn tundra, a cow moose forages in a shallow pond near the Alaska Range in Denali National Park. Moose are the most aquatic of the deer family, often submerging completely when feeding.

This page: A bull moose feeding on aquatic vegetation comes up for a breath and a look around, startling a phalarope – a small shorebird – feeding on the insect larvae that the moose's activity has stirred up.

Above: The breeding season for the moose—as with the rest of their life cycle—takes place on the margins of north country lakes and bogs. Here, a large bull sniffs the air near a cow, testing her receptiveness before mating. *Right:* During the rut, bull moose are irritable and unpredictable, and fights between males often break out. In this case, a young bull has taken on a larger, more mature male who will undoubtedly win the battle.

Far north, on the glacial lakes and ponds of Canada and the northern U.S., seasons bring radical change to the wetlands environment. During the summer, these lakes support loons, ducks, geese, and other migratory birds.

Left: Saddled with an unfortunate name, the muskrat is no rat at all, but is related to the vole. Its fur has two layers—shiny brown guard hairs, and a thick layer of dense, bluish undercoat that traps air when the muskrat dives. Muskrats are found in streams, ponds and marshes over most of North America. *Below:* With dainty nibbles, a beaver strips the tender bark from a twig. Beavers are the largest rodents in North America, with big males tipping the scales at 60 pounds.

Rich stands of aquatic plants grow in their shallow, warmer coves, attracting moose.

Weighing up to 1,200 pounds, moose are the largest members of the deer family, and they rely on the abundant food supply they find below the surface of the water to support their bulk. Through the spring, summer and fall, a moose may spend the majority of its time in the water, sometimes submerging completely as it feeds. During the dreaded blackfly season of early summer, when hordes of biting insects fill the air, the water also provides a respite from their unceasing attacks.

In a broad swath across the northern central U.S. and Canadian prairie provinces, the glaciers created a different sort of wetland – the prairie potholes. Characterized by shallow ponds distributed across the rolling plains, the pothole region has long been known as North America's "duck factory." With good reason: As many as 70 percent of the continent's waterfowl

Above: On an unusual daytime foray, a raccoon looks for food along the edge of a pond. Raccoons are found from Canada to the Mexican border, and from coast to coast, especially along waterways. *Right:* The raccoon is sometimes known as "the washer," because of its habit of playing with its food in the water. Some biologists believe that the water heightens feeling in the raccoon's soft, sensitive paws.

Above: **A beaver adds another aspen branch to its underwater larder.** *Below:* **Beavers are among the few animals that modify their environment to suit themselves, building dams for protection from predators, and digging channels that lead to rich food supplies—in this case, a flooded stand of willows.**

breed in these pools, along with shorebirds, waders, gamebirds and an incredible diversity of smaller animals.

For most of these birds, the potholes are the final destination in a long migration. Ducks and geese will have wintered along the Gulf Coast, or in the Southwest at refuges like New Mexico's Bosque del Apache. Black terns will have come from the coasts of Central and South America; Wilson's phalarope, a tiny species of shorebird, will have journeyed from the altiplano of Chile and Argentina, hopscotching north from wetland to wetland until it returns to the region of its birth, often to the same pothole.

Unfortunately, the pothole region has fallen on hard times. For more than a century, potholes have either been drained by farmers eager for more land to plow, polluted by agricultural runoff or degraded by the removal of cover along the water's edge. The rate of drainage and destruction of the potholes has been so severe that, overall, more than half are gone; in some regions the total is closer to 80 percent. In drought years, many of the remaining potholes dry up, leaving the ducks and geese with nowhere to nest.

The destruction of the prairie potholes echoes the larger problem of wetlands protection. Historically, swamps, marshes and the like were regarded as "wasteland" suitable for nothing, unless they could be drained. Tidal

Above: Rippling the reflected colors of fall, a river otter pokes its head above the surface of a pond. Otters are superlative underwater hunters. *Right:* Out of the water, the otter's membership in the weasel family is clearly shown by its long body and short legs. A playful animal, it will, in winter, slide along the ice of a pond.

A green frog's golden, periscope eyes protrude above a concealing blanket of duckweed, a common aquatic plant that can cover entire ponds in a layer of green.

Top to bottom: An old male bullfrog, his yellow throat all but hidden, floats on a quiet backwater of Lake Erie near the Ontario shore. Bullfrogs mature slowly, spending several years in the tadpole stage before growing legs. Being cold-blooded, reptiles, like this painted turtle, adjust their body temperature by moving from sun to shade. Though less dependent upon open water than the frog, in early spring, the American toad heads for ponds, marshes — even roadside puddles — to breed.

marshes and estuaries were filled in for housing; marshes were drained for farmland or used as dumps. It has only been within the past 20 years that the incalculable value of wetlands has come to be recognized. They are amazingly fertile environments; an acre of coastal tidal marsh produces more biomass — plants and animals — than the best acre of Midwest cornfield.

This slow awakening to the worth of wetlands has brought a change in attitudes. Government agencies that once championed wetlands destruction now enforce laws protecting them, although public awareness grows at a slower pace. In some areas, as will be seen in the case of southern Florida, people are even trying to undo past wrongs.

Preceding page: A golden morning fog envelopes a flock of snow geese and ducks, resting in these artificial ponds. *Above:* Canadian geese are the most recognizable and widespread of North America's native geese. *Below:* Neck tucked, a resting Canada goose nonetheless keeps a wary eye for danger. Even when a flock is feeding, several sentries at the edge of the group watch for predators.

Not all bodies of water are a remnant of the glaciers; in the north, some are the handiwork of beavers, one of the few animals to change its environment to suit its own needs. By damming streams to form deep ponds, the beaver creates a safe haven from predators, especially once its dome-shaped lodge with underwater entrances has been completed. When the

Left: Flexing its huge wings, a tundra swan runs along the surface of a river, building enough speed to take flight. Tundra swans nest in the Arctic from Alaska to Ontario, taking advantage of the constant northern sunlight and abundant insect life to raise their cygnets to quick maturity. *Below:* Tundra swans rest and preen during a stop in the Pacific Northwest. There are two populations in North America – a western group that winters along the Pacific coast and Southwest, and a smaller eastern population that flies all the way to the Atlantic seaboard, from New Jersey to the Carolinas.

winter ice seals the pond, the beaver is utterly safe from attack until the spring thaw. To tide it over these lean months, the beaver colony will have made large, underwater caches of tender aspen and willow branches, cut as needed and carried to the lodge to eat.

In the Everglades of south Florida, the marshy environment that usually occupies only a narrow skirt around a lake is expanded to encompass the lower third of the state, a vast sheet of shallow water slowly flowing through wet savannas of saw-grass. The flow of the Everglades changes with the summer rains and winter droughts.

In this flat world, the difference of an inch or two in elevation causes dramatic changes in habitat. Where the land rises slightly above the water level, saw-grass is replaced by palmettos, palms or hardwoods, a haven for bobcats or the endangered Florida panther.

Top to bottom: **Mallards are found over all of North America, Europe and most of Asia; they also migrate worldwide. Although this male mallard seems to dip its feet tentatively in a frozen pond, waterfowl feet hardly feel the cold. Two mallard drakes "tip up," gathering seeds, roots, aquatic plants and insects from the bottom. Leaving a splash behind him, a mallard drake explodes from the surface.**

The Lake Okeechobee/ Everglades water system has been severely disrupted by human development. By channelizing rivers, fouling the water with agricultural residues, tapping the flow for irrigation and drinking, and blocking it with ill-conceived roads and ditches, people have radically changed what was once a smoothly flowing waterway that drained central Florida south through the Everglades. The results have been devastating for wildlife; wading birds like herons and egrets have declined by as much as 90 percent. Now while bold plans are being laid to restore the original, natural waterflow, only time will tell if the initiative will succeed.

While fecundity in warm climates is expected, few visitors to the polar regions expect the teeming life found along its coasts. The reason for this vitality is the cold, nutrient-rich waters offshore which support plankton and

fish, which in turn support birds and mammals in a long, intricate food chain.

The great seabird colonies of the northern Atlantic and Pacific stagger the mind. Literally every ledge and cranny on a soaring cliff face will be taken over by birds: puffins with their multicolored beaks, murres and razorbills in somber black and white, auklets and murrelets and guillemots by the thousands. Kittiwakes (a species of small white gull) may carry clumps of seaweed to the ledges to build a cup for their eggs, but most of the birds incubate on the barren rock, holding their egg in place to keep it from rolling off into several hundred feet of open air. The noise is a constant, indescribable din, and the odor of fishy guano is even worse. But it is the sight, not the smell, that takes one's breath away.

Above: **Two dowitchers probe the fertile mud of a tidal flat, looking for invertebrates. Each species of shorebird is specialized to fill a unique, food-gathering niche. Known as "resource partitioning" by scientists, it keeps the species from competing directly with each other.** *Left:* **A horned grebe sits on the low-floating nest of marsh vegetation that it gathered on an Alaskan pond. Grebes are an ancient family of birds, built for diving. They are capable of sinking without a ripple and pursuing aquatic life with strong kicks of their lobed feet.** *Opposite:* **Through ruby-red eyes, a western grebe, the largest of its kind in North America, glares out at its world.**

An adult bald eagle skims low across the water, talons outstretched; with a deft snatch, it grabs a fish that had been swimming near the surface.

Bald eagles are primarily fish eaters, especially during the large salmon runs in the Pacific Northwest and Alaska.

The low northern sun glints off the tusks of an old bull walrus. The Pacific walrus is an enormous seal, with large males weighing more than a ton. *Opposite:* Walruses doze or spar with rivals on the beach of Alaska's Round Island, an important haven for the species.

At first glance the northern auks – like murres and puffins – resemble penguins. But there is no relationship: both groups have evolved from different ancestral stock, adapting in similar ways to similar environments in a process called convergent evolution. The members of the auk family (with the exception of the now-extinct great auk) have retained their ability to fly, although it takes much exertion from their down-sized wings.

Penguins, though, have thrown their lot completely with the water, exchanging the ability to fly for the ability to swim; their compact wings function as flippers, propelling them through the water with the agility of seals.

Penguins are very much animals of the water's edge, coming ashore to rest and breed, but doing all of their feeding in the cold waters close at hand. Most time their breeding with austral summer,

A herd of sea lions cavorts in the offshore chop. Highly social animals, sea lions have been reviled by commercial fishermen because they sometimes take fish from nets. *Left:* A northern elephant seal hauls up on shore. These animals can reach lengths of up to 20 feet.

Above: Water is a natural element for this most maritime of bears. The polar bear spends the majority of its life amid the shifting floes and open leads of the Arctic pack ice. *Right:* Two polar bears engage in a shoving match, complete with growls and open-mouthed threats. Such battles occasionally turn deadly, but the bear's teeth and claws are normally reserved for its prey.

but the emperor penguin – one of the two species restricted to Antarctica itself – lays its single egg in midwinter, when temperatures drop to –70 degrees. The male incubates it on his feet while the female leaves, spending two months at sea, feeding. While she is gone, the male cannot dive to eat; he scarcely moves, losing half his weight. The female returns just as the chick hatches.

Penguins are usually associated with Antarctica, but many of the world's 17 species live far from the continent. The Galápagos penguin lives on the Equator, the lovely blue penguin in New Zealand, and many other species on such subantarctic islands as the Falklands and South Orkneys.

Life is considerably easier in the Temperate Zone, where extremes of heat and cold do not occur. Such is the case over most of Europe, where wetlands have suffered much

As ghostly white as their surroundings, two ivory gulls haunt an iceberg in Griese Fiord, in Canada's far northerly Ellesmere Island.

Opposite: Jammed together cheek by jowl, dozens of murres cram a rock ledge above the churning Bering Sea. Its cold northern waters are exceptionally rich in food, and can support the millions of seabirds, like murres, that nest on nearby coastal cliffs. *Left:* An Atlantic puffin screams at a neighbor in a breeding colony on Baccalieu Island, Newfoundland. The colorful beak sheaths are grown for the breeding season, and molt off in late summer, revealing a smaller, duller beak beneath that is carried through the winter. *Below:* The horned puffin, one of two Pacific species, superficially resembles the Atlantic puffin, but has a large, two-colored bill and prominent eye scales.

A female loggerhead turtle drags herself up a Florida beach at midnight, ready to breed. Using her hind-flippers, she excavates a deep nest in the sand and fills it with eggs, which she covers before heading back into the surf.

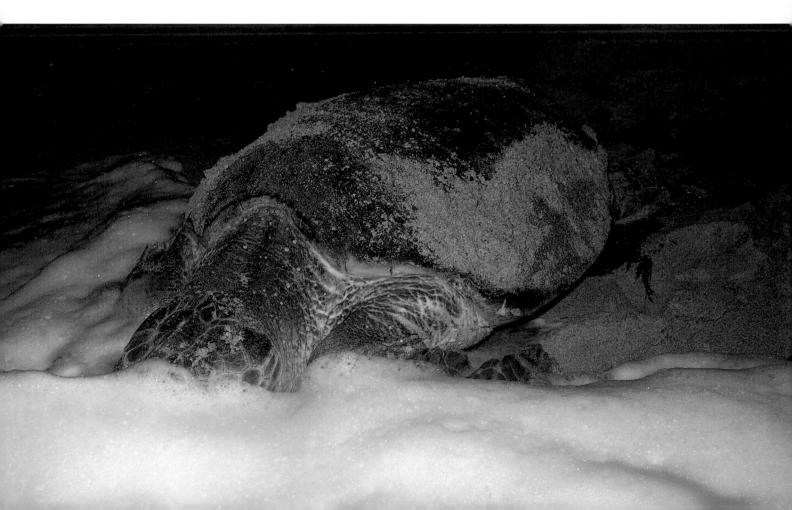

the same fate as in North America. But some jewels remain. On the French Mediterranean coast is found the Camargue, a network of marshes, lakes and salt lagoons in the Rhône River delta, home to birds and animals found nowhere else in France, like the greater flamingo. The Camarque is perhaps best-known, however, for its herds of wild white horses and black cattle – both descended from domestic stock, but gone completely feral over many generations.

After weeks of incubation in the sun, the eggs hatch at night. Hatchlings follow the shimmer of starlight on the ocean to reach the surf.

A great blue heron and a young alligator share an Everglades pool in peace — although the heron would gladly eat a newborn alligator, and a full-grown 'gator might try to catch the heron!

Springtime marshes in the Temperate Zone – Europe and North America alike – are noisy places at night. As the sun sinks, courting frogs and toads begin an ear-splitting chorus of croaks, trills and hums, all designed to attract mates. Some of the amphibians will stay near the water all summer, while many others depart after the breeding season. The quantities of eggs that they lay are astounding; some small ponds may seem all but filled with egg masses. Yet such biological extravagance is necessary, for danger is constant. No sooner are the eggs laid than predators strike: newts, leeches, diving beetles, fish and others, eagerly devour the eggs inside their gelatinous coating. Out of the remaining eggs, tadpoles hatch quickly, but they, too, fall prey. In the end, only a bare handful will survive to adulthood and return to the marsh to repeat the cycle.

Above: **A big alligator presides over his waterhole among the cypress trees. Such pools, carved by alligators during times of drought, serve as arks for Everglades wildlife when other water supplies dry up.** *Right:* **A mat of duckweed conspires to hide an already well-camouflaged alligator. Once threatened by poachers, alligators have increased in numbers so dramatically that controlled hunting seasons are now needed to keep their population in check.**

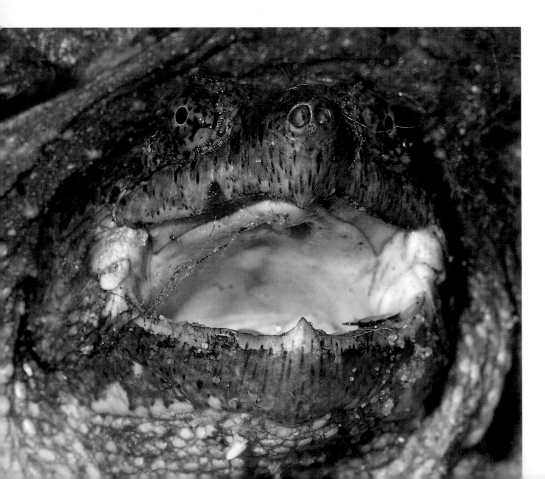

This page: Uncharacteristically exposed, a snapping turtle tries to bury itself in the mud of a pond. Snappers, while efficient predators on ducklings and fish, more often feed on carrion gleaned from the pond bottom. Their sharp jaws, while worthy of respect, cannot sever broom handles, as legend would have it.
Opposite: A great blue heron crouches low, ready to lance forward and grab a passing fish. Herons do not use their rapier beaks as spears, but instead grasp fish sideways, then toss them around to swallow headfirst.

Water takes on supreme importance for animals living in the world's more arid regions. In the deserts where standing water may be absent altogether, wildlife rely on the moisture in plants, or from the night's dew, to survive; and in the Namib Desert of Africa, certain species of long-legged beetles creep to the tops of sand dunes and wait, each night, for the fog-laden sea breeze to move in from the ocean. They cock their tails up into the draft and let the condensing fog run down their legs and into their mouths.

In other parts of Africa, water comes on a seasonal basis. The rains arrive on boiling thunderheads, and the

Opposite: **The diaphanous courtship plumes (known as aigrettes) of a great egret were once considered the height of fashion, leading to both a slaughter of egrets at the turn of the century and the birth of the National Audubon Society.** *This page:* **Lost in its own splash, a snowy egret's head temporarily disappears as it stabs downward for a fish. Smaller than the great egret, the snowy egret is known as "the bird with the golden slippers" because of its brightly colored feet. A sunfish slides down the hatch as an anhinga makes a meal of it. A marriage of exquisite color and ungainly form, a roseate spoonbill stalks the tidal waters of Ding Darling National Wildlife Refuge in Florida.**

Preceding page: Statuesque in the dusk, a flock of great egrets creates a tableau of light and dark in an inland marsh. *Above:* Cattle egrets shadow the footsteps of a wild horse in the Camargue marshes of southern France. Descended from domestic stock, the white Camargue horses live a completely wild life, sharing the vast wetland with herds of wild black cattle.

Above: Persecuted for centuries, and now suffering the ill effects of water pollution, the European river otter is declining over much of its wide range. It remains common, however, in wilder areas and along the coasts. *Left:* A European grass snake holds a struggling frog, which it will swallow headfirst. Because the snake cannot chew, it must eat its prey whole; to accommodate a large meal, the snake's lower jaws unhinge to allow its mouth to stretch to amazing proportions.

Hordes of frogs crowd a shallow breeding pool in Europe. Because many species lay their eggs in pools formed by melting snow and rain, they are at greater risk from the effects of acid rain — which is thought to be responsible for declines in frog populations in several parts of the world — than those breeding in permanent ponds.

grass savannas respond with a rush of growth. Almost overnight waterholes fill, and the plains are blanketed with lush grasses. The great herds of plant-eaters find living easy by following the rains, moving constantly across the landscape to find better graze. They cannot linger; after the rains cease, the broiling sun reduces the land to sere, brown dryness.

The waterholes remain, however, a lifeline for the wildlife. The waterhole becomes the focus of existence, drawing in zebras, antelopes, elephants and rhinos. With the grass-eaters, of course, come the meat-eaters. The waterhole is at once the giver of life and the taker, the perfect spot for an ambush. The drinking animals are constantly alert, and false alarms are a way of life.

Opposite: Among the heaviest flying birds in the world, mute swans may reach 50 pounds. They have been a sign of European royalty for centuries. Here, a mute swan graces the edge of its large nest. Its curved neck and raised wings are actually a sign of threat. *Left:* A European gray heron, a very close relative of the North American great blue heron, sits quietly in a marsh among reeds dead with the winter cold. *Below:* A male and a female white stork display at their bulky nest to reaffirm their pair bond. Storks are common birds of the European farmland, frequently nesting on rooftops—a symbol of good luck, in the eyes of many people.

Opposite page: Three hippos graze along the headwaters of the Nile River in Uganda, an activity usually restricted to nighttime hours. Clumps of water lettuce decorate the broad backs of hippos in Zambia. Docile only in appearance, hippos can be aggressive and dangerous both to each other and to humans that approach too closely. *Above:* A female black rhino and her calf cautiously sip from a waterhole; the zebras will bark a warning if lions approach.

Opposite: A lion and lioness, their coats matted and stained with mud, drink from a waterhole in Namibia's Etosha National Park. *Above:* Two Burchell's zebras match their striped reflection in the Ngorongoro Crater of Tanzania, the caldera of an extinct volcano that is now a major wildlife refuge. *Right:* Along the well-trampled fringe of an African waterhole, a male nyala and a warthog drink, while a gray heron watches the muddy water for a fish or frog.

Above: Seemingly in defiance of the laws of gravity, giraffes drop low for a drink at a waterhole. The muddy, grassless banks attest to the once-greater size of the waterhole, now shrinking under the fierce sun of the dry season. *Below:* A herd of waterbuck chew their cud while watching for lions in the lush Okavango Delta of Botswana, a vast wetland system.

The rivers of Africa provide a reliable source of water and, unlike the water-holes – which often dry completely before the next rains – can support wildlife that is not able to make the long journey to a new hole. Hippopotamuses (the "river horses" of the Greeks) spend most of their time eye-deep in rivers and springs. With their bulky bodies and short, flat-footed legs, hippos would not seem to be especially well-suited to life underwater, but they swim with an elegant grace. Comical in appearance, hippos are respected as dangerous, unpredictable animals armed with massive

Visitors to the waterholes: At right, a baboon perches on a rock for a sip of the precious liquid; below, an elephant calf stays near its mother and "aunts." Because waterholes attract so many herbivores, they are a natural spot for a lion or leopard ambush.

Monitors are common over most of Africa and Asia, and may grow to five feet long, although one species of Indonesia, the Kimodo dragon, reaches lengths of 12 feet. *Below:* Tasting the air with its long tongue, the Nile monitor searches for eggs, small animals and carrion that it may find along the shores of a river.

Nile crocodiles lounge in the sun on a sandy river bank. The croc is both predator and scavenger, grabbing unwary animals (and more than a few people) in its powerful jaws, and holding them underwater until they drown.

tusks, especially formidable if encountered when they come ashore at night to graze.

Far more deadly, however, are the crocodiles that haunt Africa's rivers. Nile crocodiles regularly reach lengths of 15 feet, and there are many reports (most undocumented) of 20-footers. There is no doubt, however, that crocodiles are dangerous to humans: on one Zambian lake alone, as many as 30 villagers were killed per month in the early 1980's.

Not yet as beautifully pink as their parents, young flamingos feed en masse, sweeping their unique bent bills through the water and filtering out tiny organisms.

This page: Three of Africa's strangest birds are found along this water's edge: At top, a pair of crowned cranes sport their tufts of yellow feathers, topping a beautiful mix of gray, black, white and red. Middle, the marabou stork's 12-foot wingspan places it among the largest birds in the world. At bottom is the shoebill stork, or whalehead, which uses its huge beak to capture fish.

Most crocodiles restrict themselves to waterbuck and other hooved species, stalking underwater until close to the drinking animal. Making a lightning-fast rush, the crocodile grabs the legs or head and drags its prey underwater. The struggling animal is held down until it drowns, then cached for later eating.

In this century, crocodiles have had as much to fear from humans as humans from them. The demand for reptilian leather put tremendous pressure on crocodilians worldwide, and many species declined to alarming levels.

The American crocodile is critically endangered, but protection has brought the American alligator back from endangered-species status to

An African fish eagle, resplendent in its chocolate-and-white plumage, sweeps low over the Okavango Delta looking for fish, then perches with its mate on a dead snag. The fish eagle's scientific name, *Haliaeetus vocifer,* refers to its loud, ringing cry. *Opposite:* The saddle-billed stork in Kenya's Masi Mara region is one of the most colorful of the world's storks.

A water monitor from Australia lashes its tail at an intruder, although the large lizard is more bluff than fight.

Jaws open in the midday heat, a saltwater crocodile basks in Australia's Northern Territory, where these giant reptiles are feared for their attacks on humans. The largest crocodiles in the world, "salties" reach lengths of more than 20 feet, with one 28-foot monster on record. *At right:* A "water-dragon," an Australian lizard.

relative abundance – so much so that legal hunting seasons are being used to control its numbers today. Protection has also helped the Nile crocodile and the saltwater crocodile of Australia, both of which had been decimated by uncontrolled shooting.

Perhaps the decline and recovery of the crocodile worldwide is an analogy to our view of wetlands as a whole. Just as we have come to realize the worth of all animals – even those that sometimes kill people – so have we come to a better understanding of their home. Marshes, swamps and the like might not be prime real estate in the conventional sense, but they have value that transcends human use. They are a vital link in the chain of life, important beyond their size, and far beyond their watery borders.

Two eastern gray kangaroos are silhouetted by the sunrise as they pause on the beach at Cape Hillsborough National Park in Queensland. Eastern gray kangaroos occur throughout eastern Australia.

Index of Photography